# This planner belongs to:

_______________________

# Twenty-four

## January

| S | M | T | W | T | F | S |
|---|---|---|---|---|---|---|
|   | 1 | 2 | 3 | 4 | 5 | 6 |
| 7 | 8 | 9 | 10 | 11 | 12 | 13 |
| 14 | 15 | 16 | 17 | 18 | 19 | 20 |
| 21 | 22 | 23 | 24 | 25 | 26 | 27 |
| 28 | 29 | 30 | 31 |   |   |   |

## February

| S | M | T | W | T | F | S |
|---|---|---|---|---|---|---|
|   |   |   |   | 1 | 2 | 3 |
| 4 | 5 | 6 | 7 | 8 | 9 | 10 |
| 11 | 12 | 13 | 14 | 15 | 16 | 17 |
| 18 | 19 | 20 | 21 | 22 | 23 | 24 |
| 25 | 26 | 27 | 28 | 29 |   |   |

## March

| S | M | T | W | T | F | S |
|---|---|---|---|---|---|---|
|   |   |   |   |   | 1 | 2 |
| 3 | 4 | 5 | 6 | 7 | 8 | 9 |
| 10 | 11 | 12 | 13 | 14 | 15 | 16 |
| 17 | 18 | 19 | 20 | 21 | 22 | 23 |
| 24 | 25 | 26 | 27 | 28 | 29 | 30 |
| 31 |   |   |   |   |   |   |

## April

| S | M | T | W | T | F | S |
|---|---|---|---|---|---|---|
|   | 1 | 2 | 3 | 4 | 5 | 6 |
| 7 | 8 | 9 | 10 | 11 | 12 | 13 |
| 14 | 15 | 16 | 17 | 18 | 19 | 20 |
| 21 | 22 | 23 | 24 | 25 | 26 | 27 |
| 28 | 29 | 30 |   |   |   |   |

## May

| S | M | T | W | T | F | S |
|---|---|---|---|---|---|---|
|   |   |   | 1 | 2 | 3 | 4 |
| 5 | 6 | 7 | 8 | 9 | 10 | 11 |
| 12 | 13 | 14 | 15 | 16 | 17 | 18 |
| 19 | 20 | 21 | 22 | 23 | 24 | 25 |
| 26 | 27 | 28 | 29 | 30 | 31 |   |

## June

| S | M | T | W | T | F | S |
|---|---|---|---|---|---|---|
|   |   |   |   |   |   | 1 |
| 2 | 3 | 4 | 5 | 6 | 7 | 8 |
| 9 | 10 | 11 | 12 | 13 | 14 | 15 |
| 16 | 17 | 18 | 19 | 20 | 21 | 22 |
| 23 | 24 | 25 | 26 | 27 | 28 | 29 |
| 30 |   |   |   |   |   |   |

## July

| S | M | T | W | T | F | S |
|---|---|---|---|---|---|---|
|   | 1 | 2 | 3 | 4 | 5 | 6 |
| 7 | 8 | 9 | 10 | 11 | 12 | 13 |
| 14 | 15 | 16 | 17 | 18 | 19 | 20 |
| 21 | 22 | 23 | 24 | 25 | 26 | 27 |
| 28 | 29 | 30 | 31 |   |   |   |

## August

| S | M | T | W | T | F | S |
|---|---|---|---|---|---|---|
|   |   |   |   | 1 | 2 | 3 |
| 4 | 5 | 6 | 7 | 8 | 9 | 10 |
| 11 | 12 | 13 | 14 | 15 | 16 | 17 |
| 18 | 19 | 20 | 21 | 22 | 23 | 24 |
| 25 | 26 | 27 | 28 | 29 | 30 | 31 |

## September

| S | M | T | W | T | F | S |
|---|---|---|---|---|---|---|
| 1 | 2 | 3 | 4 | 5 | 6 | 7 |
| 8 | 9 | 10 | 11 | 12 | 13 | 14 |
| 15 | 16 | 17 | 18 | 19 | 20 | 21 |
| 22 | 23 | 24 | 25 | 26 | 27 | 28 |
| 29 | 30 |   |   |   |   |   |

## October

| S | M | T | W | T | F | S |
|---|---|---|---|---|---|---|
|   |   | 1 | 2 | 3 | 4 | 5 |
| 6 | 7 | 8 | 9 | 10 | 11 | 12 |
| 13 | 14 | 15 | 16 | 17 | 18 | 19 |
| 20 | 21 | 22 | 23 | 24 | 25 | 26 |
| 27 | 28 | 29 | 30 | 31 |   |   |

## November

| S | M | T | W | T | F | S |
|---|---|---|---|---|---|---|
|   |   |   |   |   | 1 | 2 |
| 3 | 4 | 5 | 6 | 7 | 8 | 9 |
| 10 | 11 | 12 | 13 | 14 | 15 | 16 |
| 17 | 18 | 19 | 20 | 21 | 22 | 23 |
| 24 | 25 | 26 | 27 | 28 | 29 | 30 |

## December

| S | M | T | W | T | F | S |
|---|---|---|---|---|---|---|
| 1 | 2 | 3 | 4 | 5 | 6 | 7 |
| 8 | 9 | 10 | 11 | 12 | 13 | 14 |
| 15 | 16 | 17 | 18 | 19 | 20 | 21 |
| 22 | 23 | 24 | 25 | 26 | 27 | 28 |
| 29 | 30 | 31 |   |   |   |   |

# Year in Pixels

| | J | F | M | A | M | J | J | A | S | O | N | D |
|---|---|---|---|---|---|---|---|---|---|---|---|---|
| 1. | | | | | | | | | | | | |
| 2. | | | | | | | | | | | | |
| 3. | | | | | | | | | | | | |
| 4. | | | | | | | | | | | | |
| 5. | | | | | | | | | | | | |
| 6. | | | | | | | | | | | | |
| 7. | | | | | | | | | | | | |
| 8. | | | | | | | | | | | | |
| 9. | | | | | | | | | | | | |
| 10. | | | | | | | | | | | | |
| 11. | | | | | | | | | | | | |
| 12. | | | | | | | | | | | | |
| 13. | | | | | | | | | | | | |
| 14. | | | | | | | | | | | | |
| 15. | | | | | | | | | | | | |
| 16. | | | | | | | | | | | | |
| 17. | | | | | | | | | | | | |
| 18. | | | | | | | | | | | | |
| 19. | | | | | | | | | | | | |
| 20. | | | | | | | | | | | | |
| 21. | | | | | | | | | | | | |
| 22. | | | | | | | | | | | | |
| 23. | | | | | | | | | | | | |
| 24. | | | | | | | | | | | | |
| 25. | | | | | | | | | | | | |
| 26. | | | | | | | | | | | | |
| 27. | | | | | | | | | | | | |
| 28. | | | | | | | | | | | | |
| 29. | | | | | | | | | | | | |
| 30. | | | | | | | | | | | | |
| 31. | | | | | | | | | | | | |

## Color Codes

## Notes

# January



| MONDAY | TUESDAY | WEDNESDAY | THURSDAY |
| --- | --- | --- | --- |
| 1 | 2 | 3 | 4 |
| 8 | 9 | 10 | 11 |
| 15 | 16 | 17 | 18 |
| 22 | 23 | 24 | 25 |
| 29 | 30 | 31 | |

# January 2024

| FRIDAY | SATURDAY | SUNDAY | NOTES |
|---|---|---|---|
| 5 | 6 | 7 | ○ |
| | | | ○ |
| | | | ○ |
| | | | ○ |
| | | | ○ |
| 12 | 13 | 14 | ○ |
| | | | ○ |
| | | | ○ |
| | | | ○ |
| 19 | 20 | 21 | ○ |
| | | | ○ |
| | | | ○ |
| | | | ○ |
| | | | ○ |
| 26 | 27 | 28 | ○ |
| | | | ○ |
| | | | ○ |
| | | | ○ |
| | | | ○ |
| | | | NOTES |

# February 2024

| MONDAY | TUESDAY | WEDNESDAY | THURSDAY |
|---|---|---|---|
|  |  |  | 1 |
| 5 | 6 | 7 | 8 |
| 12 | 13 | 14 | 15 |
| 19 | 20 | 21 | 22 |
| 26 | 27 | 28 | 29 |

# February 2024

| FRIDAY | SATURDAY | SUNDAY | NOTES |
|---|---|---|---|
| 2 | 3 | 4 | ○ |
| 9 | 10 | 11 | ○ |
| 16 | 17 | 18 | ○ |
| 23 | 24 | 25 | ○ |
| | | | NOTES |

# March 2024

| MONDAY | TUESDAY | WEDNESDAY | THURSDAY |
|---|---|---|---|
|  |  |  |  |
| 4 | 5 | 6 | 7 |
| 11 | 12 | 13 | 14 |
| 18 | 19 | 20 | 21 |
| 25 | 26 | 27 | 28 |

# March 2024

| FRIDAY | SATURDAY | SUNDAY | NOTES |
|---|---|---|---|
| 1 | 2 | 3 | ○ |
| | | | ○ |
| | | | ○ |
| | | | ○ |
| | | | ○ |
| 8 | 9 | 10 | ○ |
| | | | ○ |
| | | | ○ |
| | | | ○ |
| 15 | 16 | 17 | ○ |
| | | | ○ |
| | | | ○ |
| | | | ○ |
| | | | ○ |
| 22 | 23 | 24 | ○ |
| | | | ○ |
| | | | ○ |
| | | | ○ |
| | | | ○ |
| 29 | 30 | 31 | NOTES |

# April 2024

| MONDAY | TUESDAY | WEDNESDAY | THURSDAY |
| --- | --- | --- | --- |
| 1 | 2 | 3 | 4 |
| 8 | 9 | 10 | 11 |
| 15 | 16 | 17 | 18 |
| 22 | 23 | 24 | 25 |
| 29 | 30 | | |

# April 2024

| FRIDAY | SATURDAY | SUNDAY | NOTES |
| --- | --- | --- | --- |
| 5 | 6 | 7 | ○ |
| | | | ○ |
| | | | ○ |
| | | | ○ |
| | | | ○ |
| 12 | 13 | 14 | ○ |
| | | | ○ |
| | | | ○ |
| | | | ○ |
| 19 | 20 | 21 | ○ |
| | | | ○ |
| | | | ○ |
| | | | ○ |
| | | | ○ |
| 26 | 27 | 28 | ○ |
| | | | ○ |
| | | | ○ |
| | | | ○ |
| | | | ○ |
| | | | NOTES |

# May 2024

| MONDAY | TUESDAY | WEDNESDAY | THURSDAY |
|---|---|---|---|
|  |  | 1 | 2 |
| 6 | 7 | 8 | 9 |
| 13 | 14 | 15 | 16 |
| 20 | 21 | 22 | 23 |
| 27 | 28 | 29 | 30 |

# May 2024

| FRIDAY | SATURDAY | SUNDAY | NOTES |
|---|---|---|---|
| 3 | 4 | 5 | ○ |
|  |  |  | ○ |
|  |  |  | ○ |
|  |  |  | ○ |
|  |  |  | ○ |
| 10 | 11 | 12 | ○ |
|  |  |  | ○ |
|  |  |  | ○ |
|  |  |  | ○ |
| 17 | 18 | 19 | ○ |
|  |  |  | ○ |
|  |  |  | ○ |
|  |  |  | ○ |
|  |  |  | ○ |
| 24 | 25 | 26 | ○ |
|  |  |  | ○ |
|  |  |  | ○ |
|  |  |  | ○ |
|  |  |  | ○ |
| 31 |  |  | NOTES |

# June 2024

| MONDAY | TUESDAY | WEDNESDAY | THURSDAY |
|---|---|---|---|
|  |  |  |  |
| 3 | 4 | 5 | 6 |
| 10 | 11 | 12 | 13 |
| 17 | 18 | 19 | 20 |
| 24 | 25 | 26 | 27 |

# June 2024

| FRIDAY | SATURDAY | SUNDAY | NOTES |
|---|---|---|---|
| | 1 | 2 | ○ |
| | | | ○ |
| | | | ○ |
| | | | ○ |
| | | | ○ |
| 7 | 8 | 9 | ○ |
| | | | ○ |
| | | | ○ |
| | | | ○ |
| | | | ○ |
| 14 | 15 | 16 | ○ |
| | | | ○ |
| | | | ○ |
| | | | ○ |
| | | | ○ |
| 21 | 22 | 23 | ○ |
| | | | ○ |
| | | | ○ |
| | | | ○ |
| | | | ○ |
| 28 | 29 | 30 | NOTES |

# July 2024

| MONDAY | TUESDAY | WEDNESDAY | THURSDAY |
|---|---|---|---|
| 1 | 2 | 3 | 4 |
| 8 | 9 | 10 | 11 |
| 15 | 16 | 17 | 18 |
| 22 | 23 | 24 | 25 |
| 29 | 30 | 31 |  |

# July 2024

| FRIDAY | SATURDAY | SUNDAY | NOTES |
|---|---|---|---|
| 5 | 6 | 7 | ○ |
| | | | ○ |
| | | | ○ |
| | | | ○ |
| | | | ○ |
| 12 | 13 | 14 | ○ |
| | | | ○ |
| | | | ○ |
| | | | ○ |
| 19 | 20 | 21 | ○ |
| | | | ○ |
| | | | ○ |
| | | | ○ |
| | | | ○ |
| 26 | 27 | 28 | ○ |
| | | | ○ |
| | | | ○ |
| | | | ○ |
| | | | ○ |
| | | | NOTES |

# August 2024

| MONDAY | TUESDAY | WEDNESDAY | THURSDAY |
|---|---|---|---|
|  |  |  | 1 |
| 5 | 6 | 7 | 8 |
| 12 | 13 | 14 | 15 |
| 19 | 20 | 21 | 22 |
| 26 | 27 | 28 | 29 |

# August 2024

| FRIDAY | SATURDAY | SUNDAY | NOTES |
|---|---|---|---|
| 2 | 3 | 4 | ○ |
| 9 | 10 | 11 | ○ |
| 16 | 17 | 18 | ○ |
| 23 | 24 | 25 | ○ |
| 30 | 31 |  | NOTES |

# September 2024

| MONDAY | TUESDAY | WEDNESDAY | THURSDAY |
|---|---|---|---|
|  |  |  |  |
| 2 | 3 | 4 | 5 |
| 9 | 10 | 11 | 12 |
| 16 | 17 | 18 | 19 |
| 23 | 24 | 25 | 26 |

# September 2024

| FRIDAY | SATURDAY | SUNDAY | NOTES |
|---|---|---|---|
|  |  | 1 | ○ |
|  |  |  | ○ |
|  |  |  | ○ |
|  |  |  | ○ |
|  |  |  | ○ |
| 6 | 7 | 8 | ○ |
|  |  |  | ○ |
|  |  |  | ○ |
|  |  |  | ○ |
| 13 | 14 | 15 | ○ |
|  |  |  | ○ |
|  |  |  | ○ |
|  |  |  | ○ |
|  |  |  | ○ |
| 20 | 21 | 22 | ○ |
|  |  |  | ○ |
|  |  |  | ○ |
|  |  |  | ○ |
|  |  |  | ○ |
| 27 | 28 | 29 | 30 |

# October 2024

| MONDAY | TUESDAY | WEDNESDAY | THURSDAY |
|---|---|---|---|
|  | 1 | 2 | 3 |
| 7 | 8 | 9 | 10 |
| 14 | 15 | 16 | 17 |
| 21 | 22 | 23 | 24 |
| 28 | 29 | 30 | 31 |

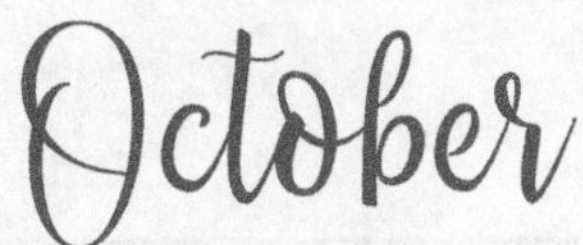

# October 2024

| FRIDAY | SATURDAY | SUNDAY | NOTES |
|---|---|---|---|
| 4 | 5 | 6 | ○ |
|  |  |  | ○ |
|  |  |  | ○ |
|  |  |  | ○ |
|  |  |  | ○ |
| 11 | 12 | 13 | ○ |
|  |  |  | ○ |
|  |  |  | ○ |
|  |  |  | ○ |
| 18 | 19 | 20 | ○ |
|  |  |  | ○ |
|  |  |  | ○ |
|  |  |  | ○ |
|  |  |  | ○ |
| 25 | 26 | 27 | ○ |
|  |  |  | ○ |
|  |  |  | ○ |
|  |  |  | ○ |
|  |  |  | ○ |
|  |  |  | NOTES |

# November 2024

| MONDAY | TUESDAY | WEDNESDAY | THURSDAY |
|---|---|---|---|
|  |  |  |  |
| 4 | 5 | 6 | 7 |
| 11 | 12 | 13 | 14 |
| 18 | 19 | 20 | 21 |
| 25 | 26 | 27 | 28 |

# November 2024

| FRIDAY | SATURDAY | SUNDAY | NOTES |
|---|---|---|---|
| 1 | 2 | 3 | ○ |
| | | | ○ |
| | | | ○ |
| | | | ○ |
| | | | ○ |
| 8 | 9 | 10 | ○ |
| | | | ○ |
| | | | ○ |
| | | | ○ |
| 15 | 16 | 17 | ○ |
| | | | ○ |
| | | | ○ |
| | | | ○ |
| | | | ○ |
| 22 | 23 | 24 | ○ |
| | | | ○ |
| | | | ○ |
| | | | ○ |
| | | | ○ |
| 29 | 30 | | NOTES |

# December 2024

| MONDAY | TUESDAY | WEDNESDAY | THURSDAY |
|---|---|---|---|
|  |  |  |  |
| 2 | 3 | 4 | 5 |
| 9 | 10 | 11 | 12 |
| 16 | 17 | 18 | 19 |
| 23 | 24 | 25 | 26 |

# December 2024

| FRIDAY | SATURDAY | SUNDAY | NOTES |
|---|---|---|---|
|  |  | 1 | ○ |
|  |  |  | ○ |
| 6 | 7 | 8 | ○ |
| 13 | 14 | 15 | ○ |
| 20 | 21 | 22 | ○ |
| 27 | 28 | 29 | 30 / 31 |

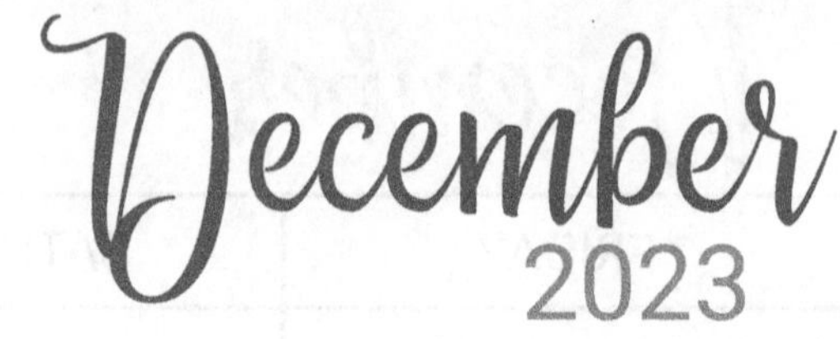


**01** FRIDAY

**02** SATURDAY

**03** SUNDAY

**04** MONDAY

**05** TUESDAY

**06** WEDNESDAY

**07** THURSDAY

**08** FRIDAY

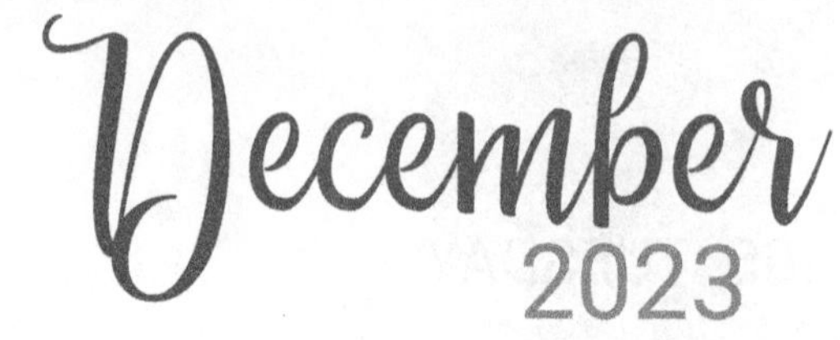



**09** SATURDAY

**10** SUNDAY

**11** MONDAY

**12** TUESDAY

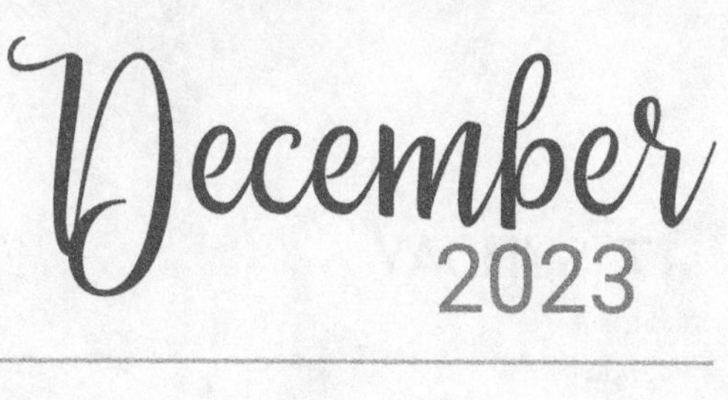

# December 2023

## 13 WEDNESDAY

## 14 THURSDAY

## 15 FRIDAY

## 16 SATURDAY

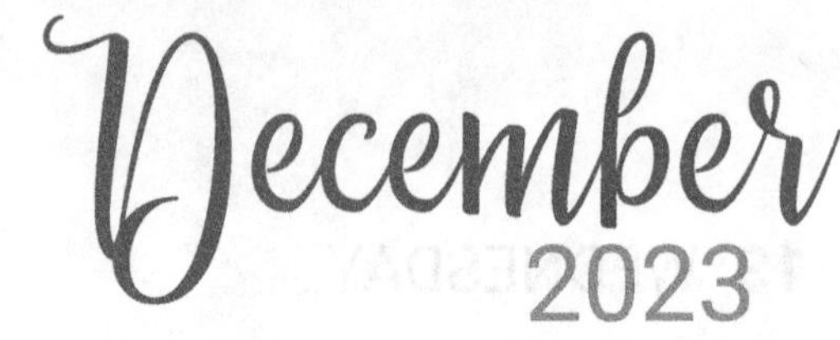

# December
## 2023

**17** SUNDAY

**18** MONDAY

**19** TUESDAY

**20** WEDNESDAY

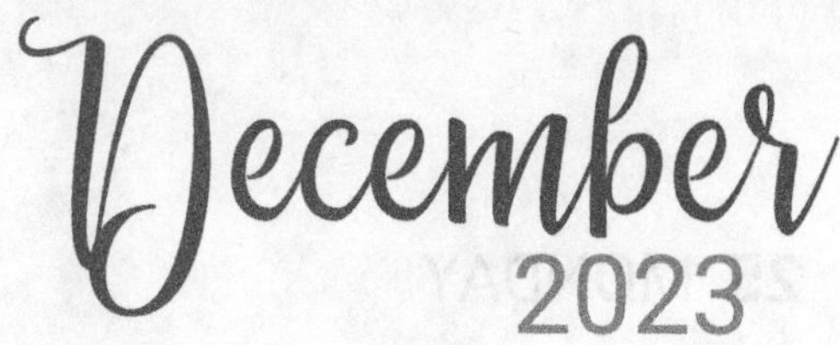

# December
## 2023

**21** THURSDAY

**22** FRIDAY

**23** SATURDAY

**24** SUNDAY

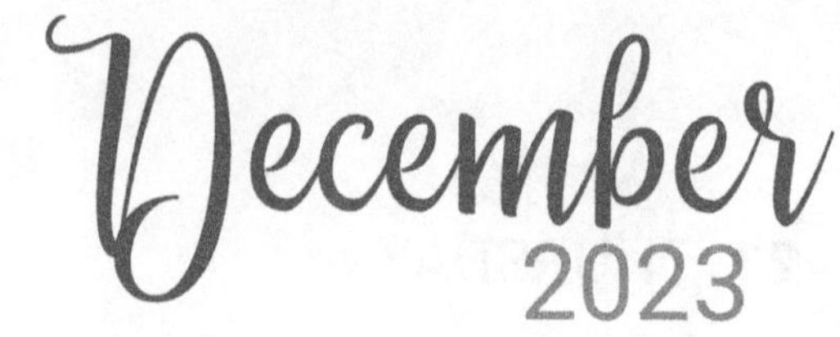



**25** MONDAY

**26** TUESDAY

**27** WEDNESDAY

**28** THURSDAY

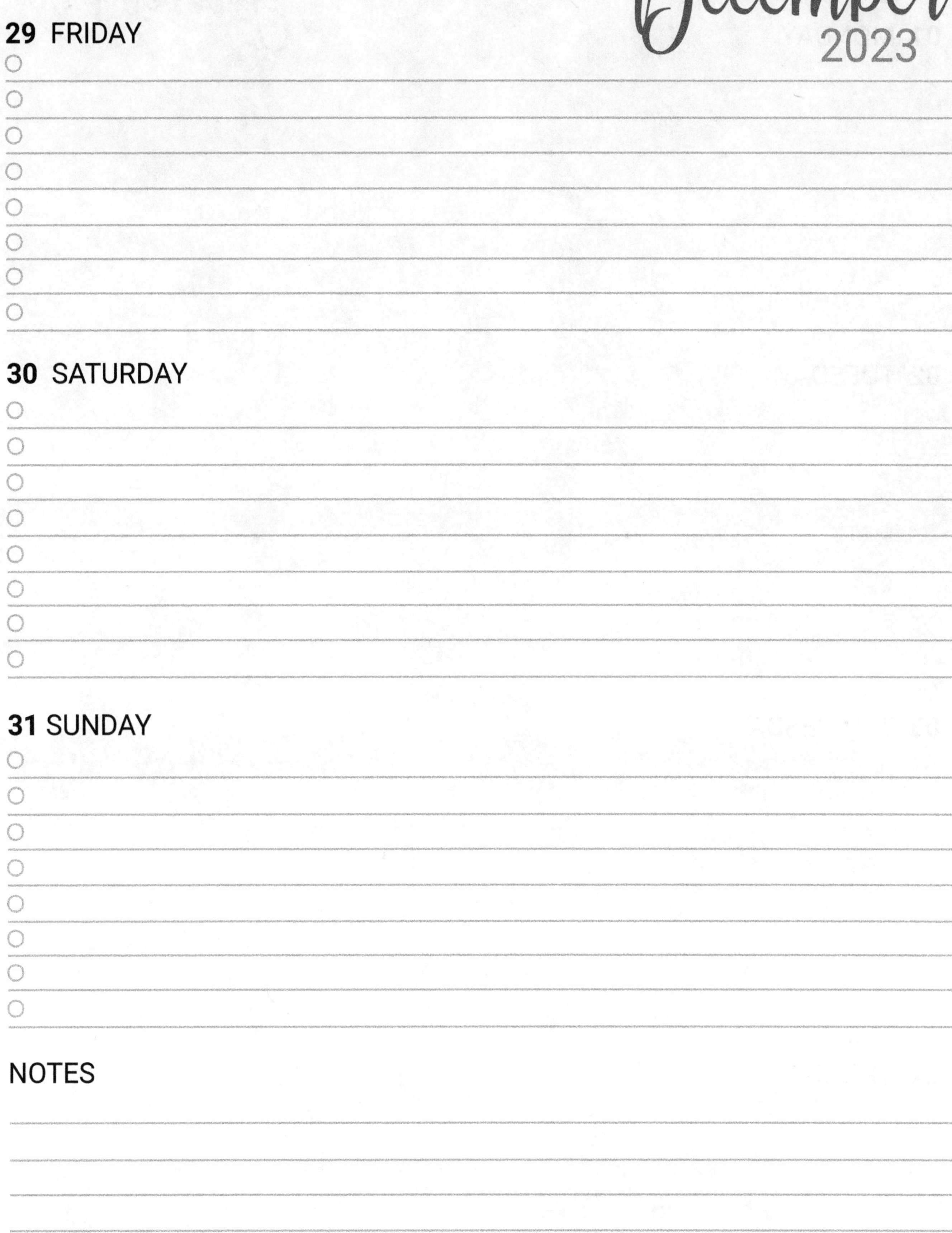


December
2023

**29** FRIDAY

**30** SATURDAY

**31** SUNDAY

NOTES

# January
## 2024

**01** MONDAY

○ ____________________
○ ____________________
○ ____________________
○ ____________________
○ ____________________
○ ____________________
○ ____________________
○ ____________________

**02** TUESDAY

○ ____________________
○ ____________________
○ ____________________
○ ____________________
○ ____________________
○ ____________________
○ ____________________
○ ____________________

**03** WEDNESDAY

○ ____________________
○ ____________________
○ ____________________
○ ____________________
○ ____________________
○ ____________________
○ ____________________
○ ____________________

**04** THURSDAY

○ ____________________
○ ____________________
○ ____________________
○ ____________________
○ ____________________

**05** FRIDAY

**06** SATURDAY

**07** SUNDAY

**08** MONDAY

**09** TUESDAY

**10** WEDNESDAY

**11** THURSDAY

**12** FRIDAY

**13** SATURDAY

**14** SUNDAY

**15** MONDAY

**16** TUESDAY

**17** WEDNESDAY

**18** THURSDAY

**19** FRIDAY

**20** SATURDAY

**21** SUNDAY

**22** MONDAY

**23** TUESDAY

**24** WEDNESDAY

**25** THURSDAY

**26** FRIDAY

**27** SATURDAY

**28** SUNDAY

## 29 MONDAY

○
○
○
○
○
○
○
○

## 30 TUESDAY

○
○
○
○
○
○
○
○

## 31 WEDNESDAY

○
○
○
○
○
○
○
○

## NOTES

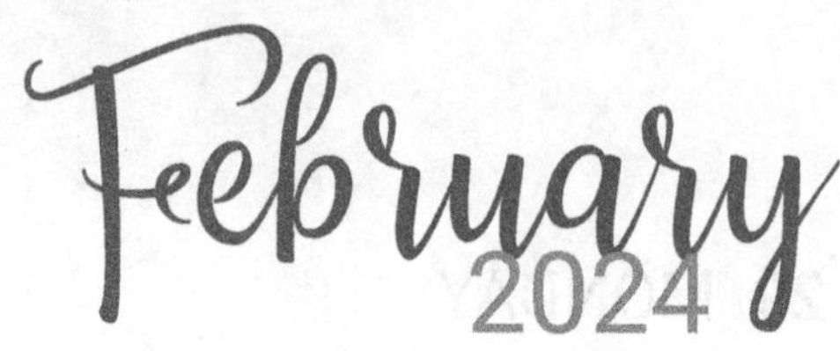


## 01 THURSDAY

- 
- 
- 
- 
- 
- 
- 

## 02 FRIDAY

- 
- 
- 
- 
- 
- 
- 
- 

## 03 SATURDAY

- 
- 
- 
- 
- 
- 
- 
- 

## 04 SUNDAY

- 
- 
- 
- 
- 

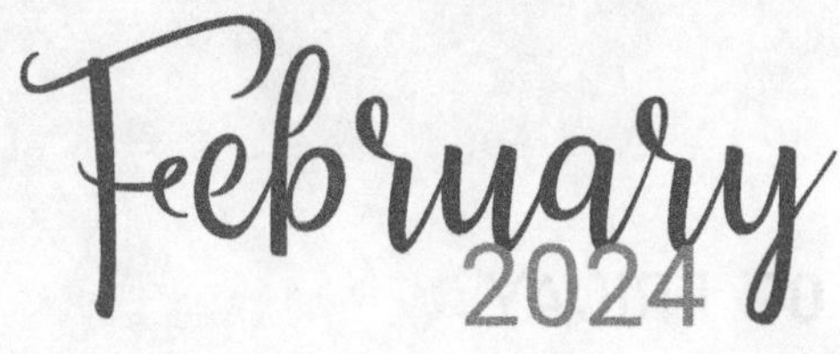

# February
## 2024

**05** MONDAY

**06** TUESDAY

**07** WEDNESDAY

**08** THURSDAY

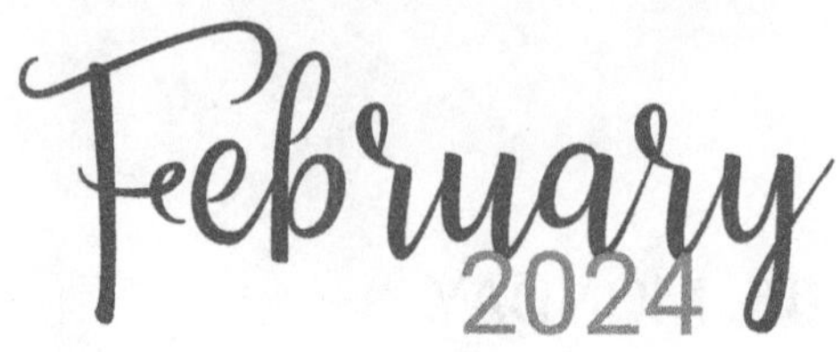



## 09 FRIDAY

○ ___________________________________________
○ ___________________________________________
○ ___________________________________________
○ ___________________________________________
○ ___________________________________________
○ ___________________________________________
○ ___________________________________________
○ ___________________________________________

## 10 SATURDAY

○ ___________________________________________
○ ___________________________________________
○ ___________________________________________
○ ___________________________________________
○ ___________________________________________
○ ___________________________________________
○ ___________________________________________
○ ___________________________________________

## 11 SUNDAY

○ ___________________________________________
○ ___________________________________________
○ ___________________________________________
○ ___________________________________________
○ ___________________________________________
○ ___________________________________________
○ ___________________________________________
○ ___________________________________________

## 12 MONDAY

○ ___________________________________________
○ ___________________________________________
○ ___________________________________________
○ ___________________________________________
○ ___________________________________________

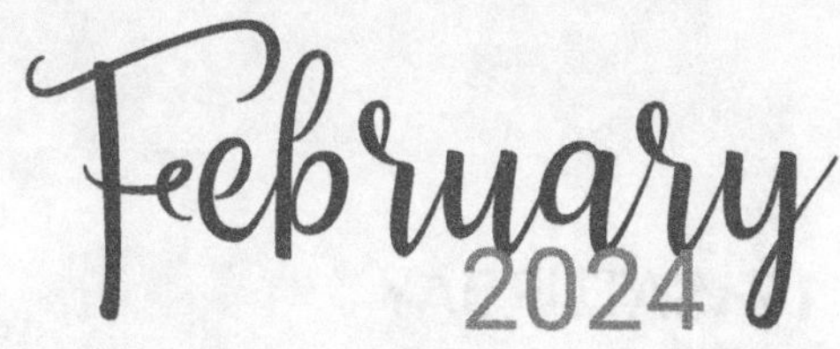

**13** TUESDAY

**14** WEDNESDAY

**15** THURSDAY

**16** FRIDAY

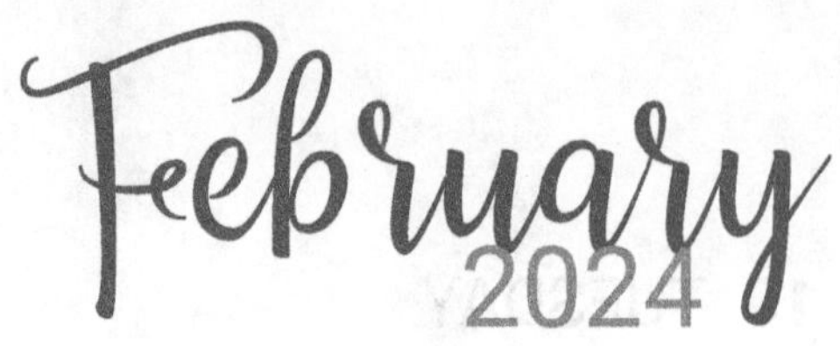


**17** SATURDAY

**18** SUNDAY

**19** MONDAY

**20** TUESDAY

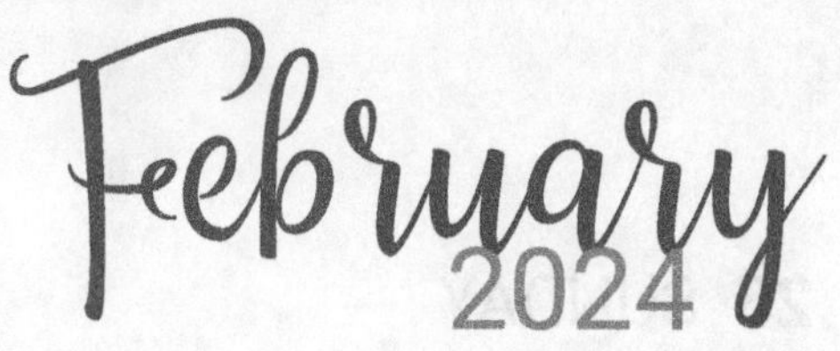


**21** WEDNESDAY

**22** THURSDAY

**23** FRIDAY

**24** SATURDAY

## 25 SUNDAY

## 26 MONDAY

## 27 TUESDAY

## 28 WEDNESDAY

**29** THURSDAY

- 
- 
- 
- 
- 
- 
- 
- 

NOTES

# March
### 2024

**01** FRIDAY

**02** SATURDAY

**03** SUNDAY

**04** MONDAY

**05** TUESDAY

**06** WEDNESDAY

**07** THURSDAY

**08** FRIDAY

**09** SATURDAY

**10** SUNDAY

**11** MONDAY

**12** TUESDAY

## 13 WEDNESDAY

## 14 THURSDAY

## 15 FRIDAY

## 16 SATURDAY

**17** SUNDAY

**18** MONDAY

**19** TUESDAY

**20** WEDNESDAY

## 21 THURSDAY

## 22 FRIDAY

## 23 SATURDAY

## 24 SUNDAY

**25** MONDAY

**26** TUESDAY

**27** WEDNESDAY

**28** THURSDAY

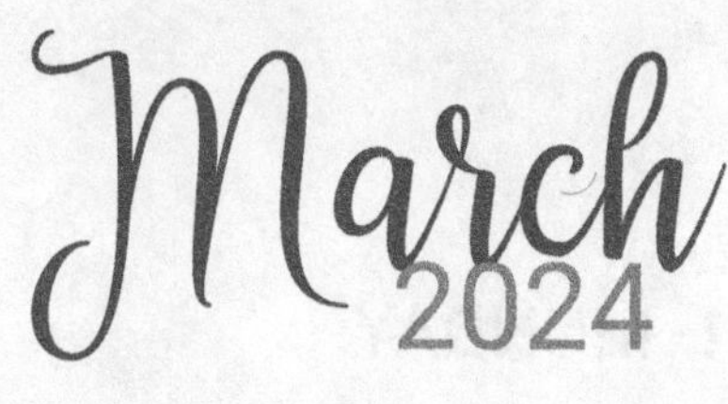



## 29 FRIDAY

○
○
○
○
○
○
○

## 30 SATURDAY

○
○
○
○
○
○
○
○

## 31 SUNDAY

○
○
○
○
○
○
○
○

## NOTES

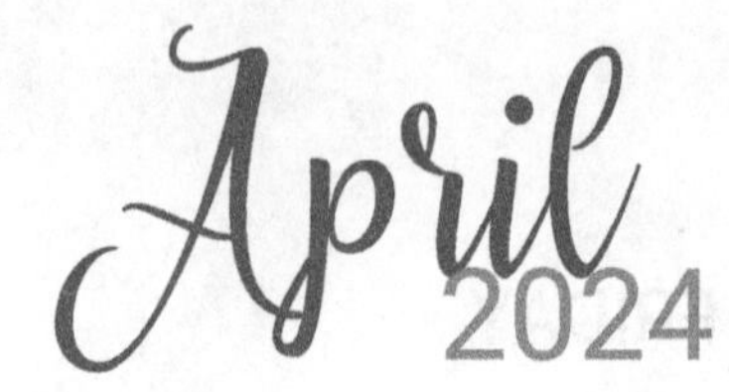

# April
## 2024

**01** MONDAY

○
○
○
○
○
○
○

**02** TUESDAY

○
○
○
○
○
○
○
○

**03** WEDNESDAY

○
○
○
○
○
○
○
○

**04** THURSDAY

○
○
○
○
○

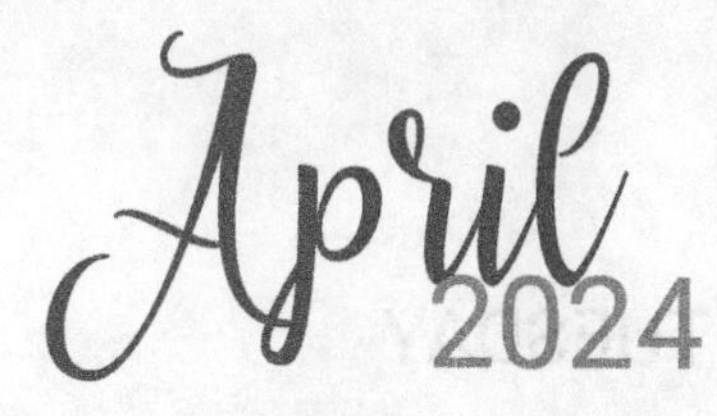


## 05 FRIDAY

## 06 SATURDAY

## 07 SUNDAY

## 08 MONDAY

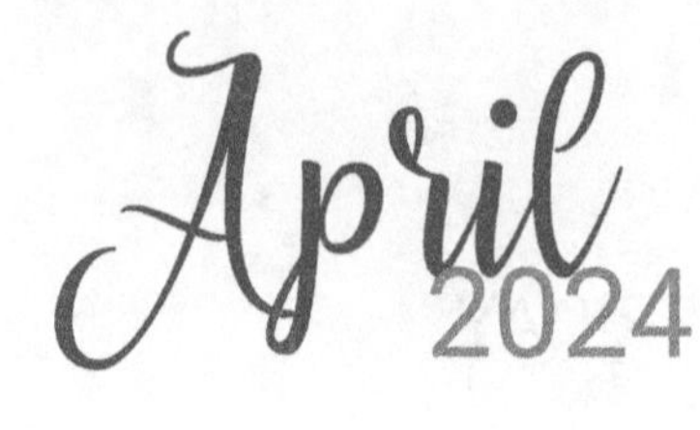

**April**
2024

**09** TUESDAY

**10** WEDNESDAY

**11** THURSDAY

**12** FRIDAY

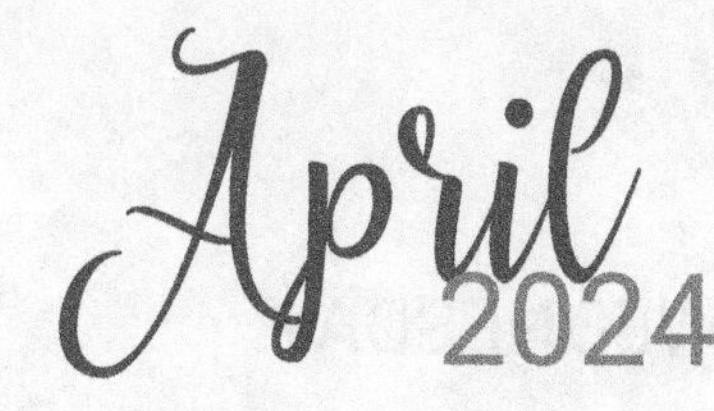

# April 2024

## 13 SATURDAY

## 14 SUNDAY

## 15 MONDAY

## 16 TUESDAY

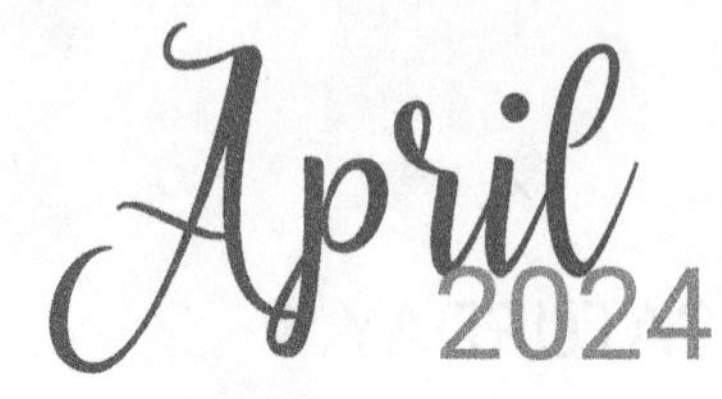


## 17 WEDNESDAY

## 18 THURSDAY

## 19 FRIDAY

## 20 SATURDAY

## 21 SUNDAY

## 22 MONDAY

## 23 TUESDAY

## 24 WEDNESDAY

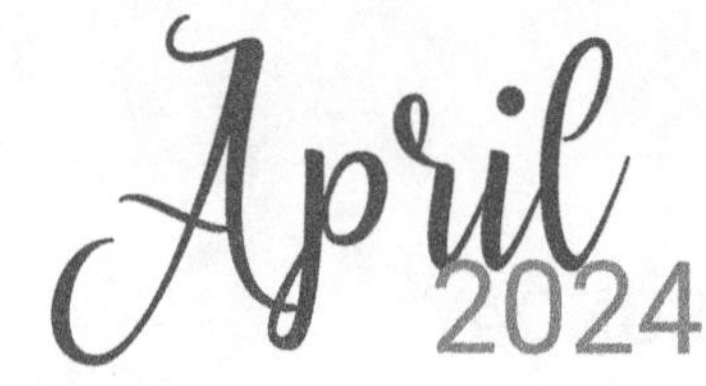



## 25 THURSDAY

## 26 FRIDAY

## 27 SATURDAY

## 28 SUNDAY

**29** MONDAY

**30** TUESDAY

NOTES

**01** WEDNESDAY

**02** THURSDAY

**03** FRIDAY

**04** SATURDAY

## 05 SUNDAY

## 06 MONDAY

## 07 TUESDAY

## 08 WEDNESDAY

# May
## 2024

## 09 THURSDAY

## 10 FRIDAY

## 11 SATURDAY

## 12 SUNDAY

**13** MONDAY

**14** TUESDAY

**15** WEDNESDAY

**16** THURSDAY

**17** FRIDAY

**18** SATURDAY

**19** SUNDAY

**20** MONDAY

## 21 TUESDAY

## 22 WEDNESDAY

## 23 THURSDAY

## 24 FRIDAY

## 25 SATURDAY

## 26 SUNDAY

## 27 MONDAY

## 28 TUESDAY

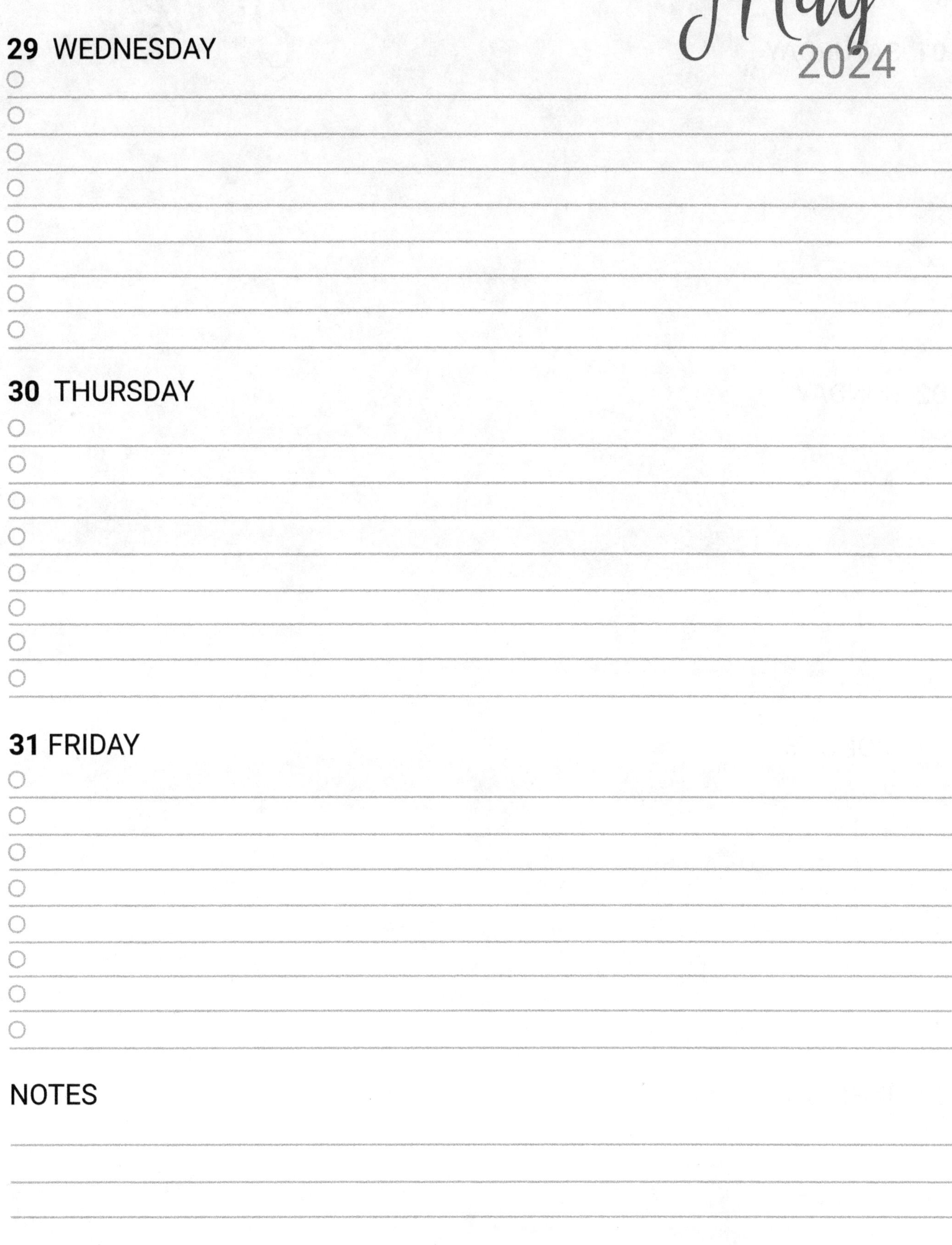



**29** WEDNESDAY

**30** THURSDAY

**31** FRIDAY

NOTES

# June
## 2024

**01** SATURDAY

○ _______________________________
○ _______________________________
○ _______________________________
○ _______________________________
○ _______________________________
○ _______________________________
○ _______________________________

**02** SUNDAY

○ _______________________________
○ _______________________________
○ _______________________________
○ _______________________________
○ _______________________________
○ _______________________________
○ _______________________________

**03** MONDAY

○ _______________________________
○ _______________________________
○ _______________________________
○ _______________________________
○ _______________________________
○ _______________________________
○ _______________________________

**04** TUESDAY

○ _______________________________
○ _______________________________
○ _______________________________
○ _______________________________
○ _______________________________

**05** WEDNESDAY

**06** THURSDAY

**07** FRIDAY

**08** SATURDAY

**09** SUNDAY

**10** MONDAY

**11** TUESDAY

**12** WEDNESDAY

## 13 THURSDAY

## 14 FRIDAY

## 15 SATURDAY

## 16 SUNDAY

**17** MONDAY

**18** TUESDAY

**19** WEDNESDAY

**20** THURSDAY

## 21 FRIDAY

## 22 SATURDAY

## 23 SUNDAY

## 24 MONDAY

**25** TUESDAY

**26** WEDNESDAY

**27** THURSDAY

**28** FRIDAY

## 29 SATURDAY

- ○
- ○
- ○
- ○
- ○
- ○
- ○
- ○

## 30 SUNDAY

- ○
- ○
- ○
- ○
- ○
- ○
- ○
- ○

## NOTES

# July
## 2024

**01** MONDAY

○
○
○
○
○
○
○
○

**02** TUESDAY

○
○
○
○
○
○
○
○

**03** WEDNESDAY

○
○
○
○
○
○
○
○

**04** THURSDAY

○
○
○
○
○

# July
## 2024

**05** FRIDAY

**06** SATURDAY

**07** SUNDAY

**08** MONDAY

# July
## 2024

**09** TUESDAY

**10** WEDNESDAY

**11** THURSDAY

**12** FRIDAY

**13** SATURDAY

**14** SUNDAY

**15** MONDAY

**16** TUESDAY

**17** WEDNESDAY

**18** THURSDAY

**19** FRIDAY

**20** SATURDAY

**21** SUNDAY

**22** MONDAY

**23** TUESDAY

**24** WEDNESDAY

**25** THURSDAY

**26** FRIDAY

**27** SATURDAY

**28** SUNDAY

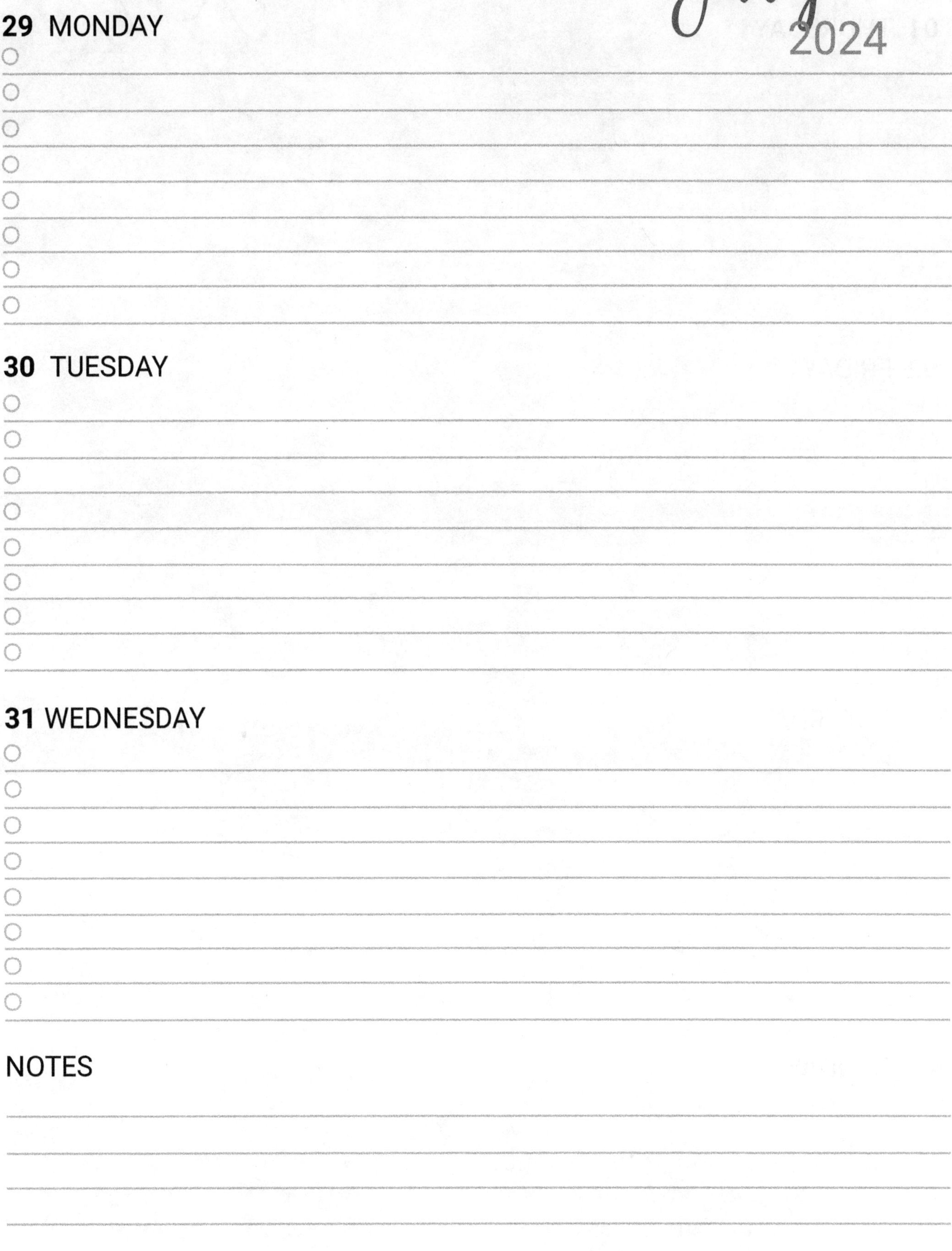


July
2024

**29** MONDAY

**30** TUESDAY

**31** WEDNESDAY

NOTES

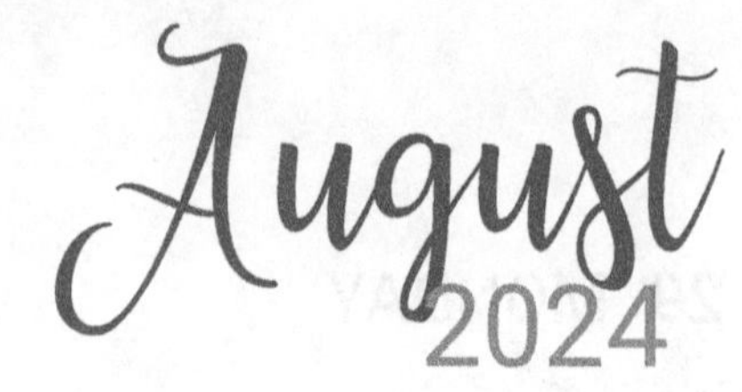


**01** THURSDAY

**02** FRIDAY

**03** SATURDAY

**04** SUNDAY

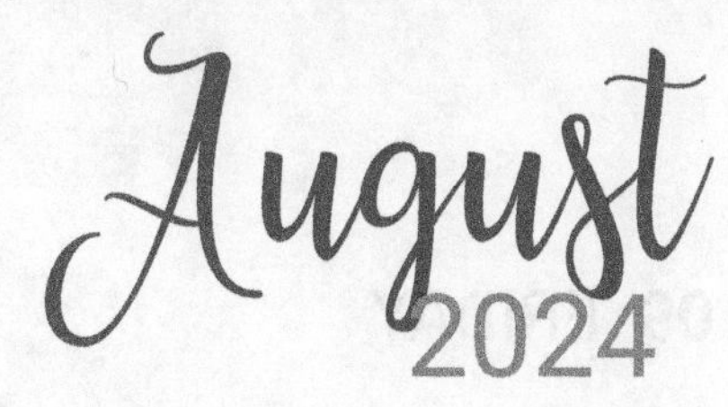

**August**
2024

**05** MONDAY

**06** TUESDAY

**07** WEDNESDAY

**08** THURSDAY

**09** FRIDAY

**10** SATURDAY

**11** SUNDAY

**12** MONDAY

## 13 TUESDAY

## 14 WEDNESDAY

## 15 THURSDAY

## 16 FRIDAY

**17** SATURDAY

- 
- 
- 
- 
- 
- 
- 

**18** SUNDAY

- 
- 
- 
- 
- 
- 
- 

**19** MONDAY

- 
- 
- 
- 
- 
- 
- 
- 

**20** TUESDAY

- 
- 
- 
- 
- 

**21** WEDNESDAY

**22** THURSDAY

**23** FRIDAY

**24** SATURDAY

**25** SUNDAY

○
○
○
○
○
○
○

**26** MONDAY

○
○
○
○
○
○
○

**27** TUESDAY

○
○
○
○
○
○
○

**28** WEDNESDAY

○
○
○
○
○

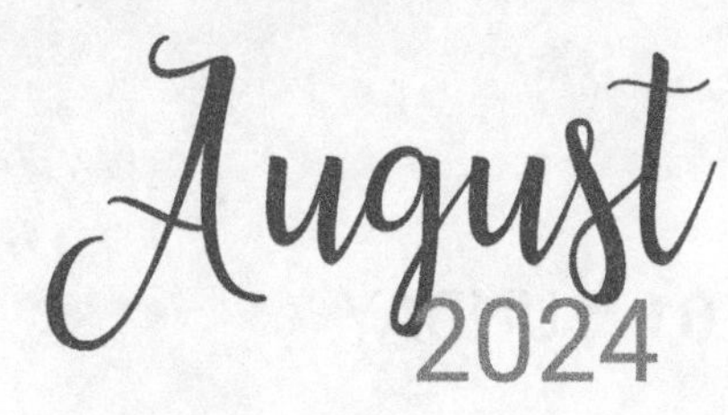

# August
## 2024

**29** THURSDAY

○

○

○

○

○

○

○

○

**30** FRIDAY

○

○

○

○

○

○

○

○

**31** SATURDAY

○

○

○

○

○

○

○

○

NOTES

# September
2024

**01** SUNDAY

**02** MONDAY

**03** TUESDAY

**04** WEDNESDAY

## 05 THURSDAY

○
○
○
○
○
○
○
○

## 06 FRIDAY

○
○
○
○
○
○
○
○

## 07 SATURDAY

○
○
○
○
○
○
○
○

## 08 SUNDAY

○
○
○
○
○

**09** MONDAY

**10** TUESDAY

**11** WEDNESDAY

**12** THURSDAY

**13** FRIDAY

**14** SATURDAY

**15** SUNDAY

**16** MONDAY

**17** TUESDAY

**18** WEDNESDAY

**19** THURSDAY

**20** FRIDAY

**21** SATURDAY

**22** SUNDAY

**23** MONDAY

**24** TUESDAY

**25** WEDNESDAY

**26** THURSDAY

**27** FRIDAY

**28** SATURDAY

**29** SUNDAY

○
○
○
○
○
○
○
○

**30** MONDAY

○
○
○
○
○
○
○
○

## NOTES

## *October*
### 2024

**01** TUESDAY

- ○
- ○
- ○
- ○
- ○
- ○
- ○
- ○

**02** WEDNESDAY

- ○
- ○
- ○
- ○
- ○
- ○
- ○
- ○

**03** THURSDAY

- ○
- ○
- ○
- ○
- ○
- ○
- ○
- ○

**04** FRIDAY

- ○
- ○
- ○
- ○
- ○

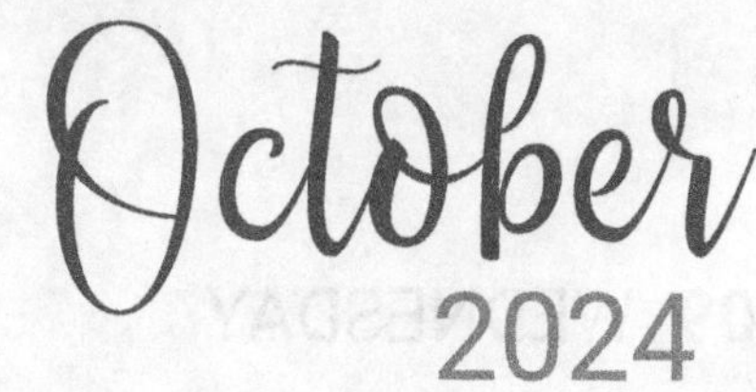



## 05 SATURDAY

## 06 SUNDAY

## 07 MONDAY

## 08 TUESDAY

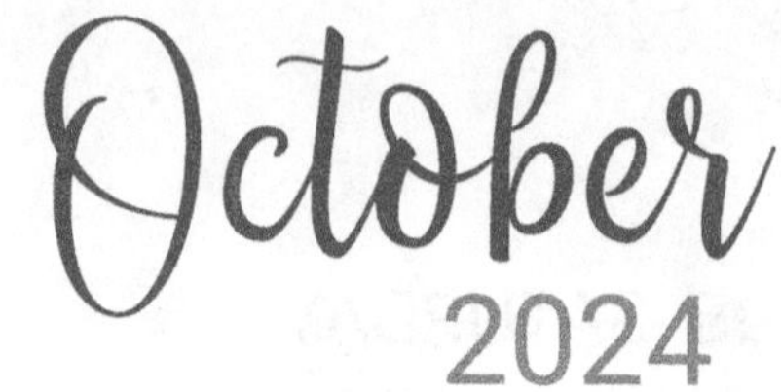

# October
## 2024

**09** WEDNESDAY

**10** THURSDAY

**11** FRIDAY

**12** SATURDAY

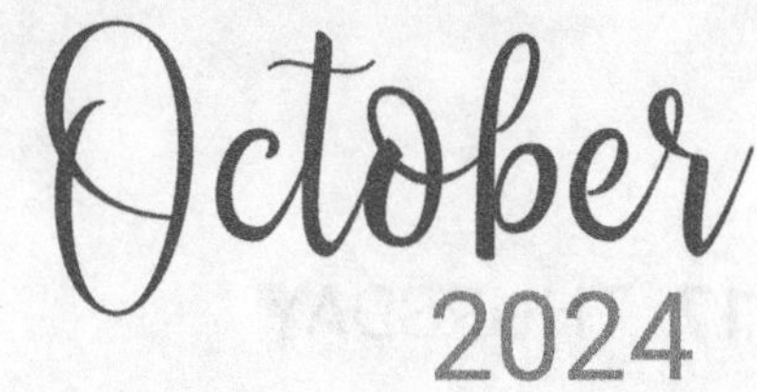

# October 2024

## 13 SUNDAY

## 14 MONDAY

## 15 TUESDAY

## 16 WEDNESDAY

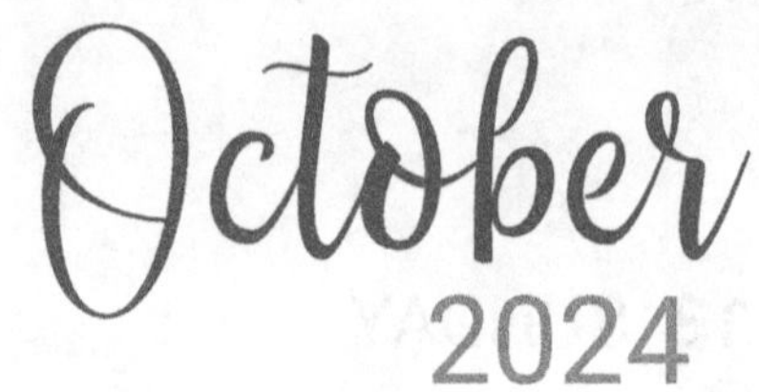

# October
## 2024

**17** THURSDAY

**18** FRIDAY

**19** SATURDAY

**20** SUNDAY

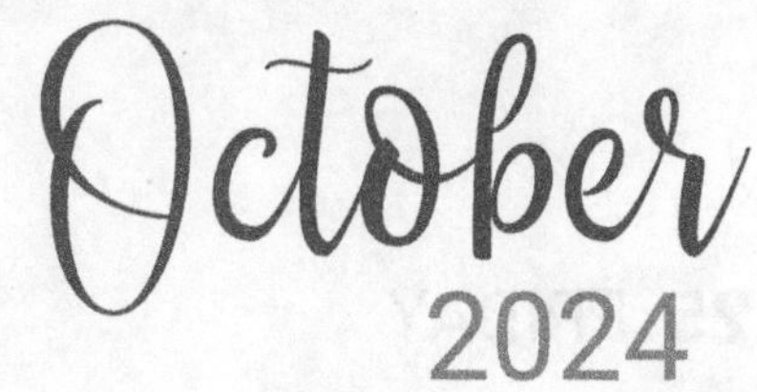

# October
## 2024

## 21 MONDAY

## 22 TUESDAY

## 23 WEDNESDAY

## 24 THURSDAY

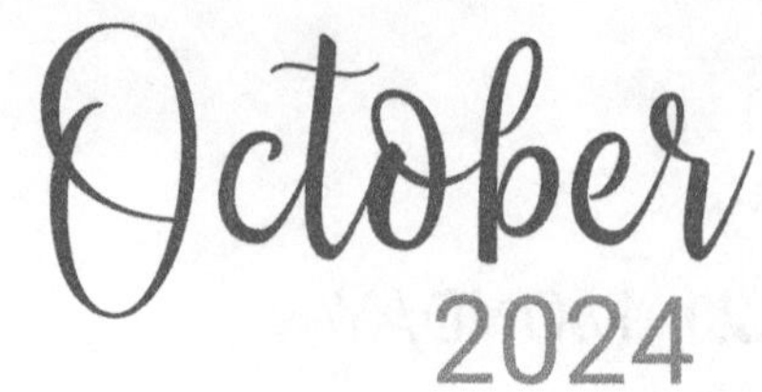



**25** FRIDAY

**26** SATURDAY

**27** SUNDAY

**28** MONDAY

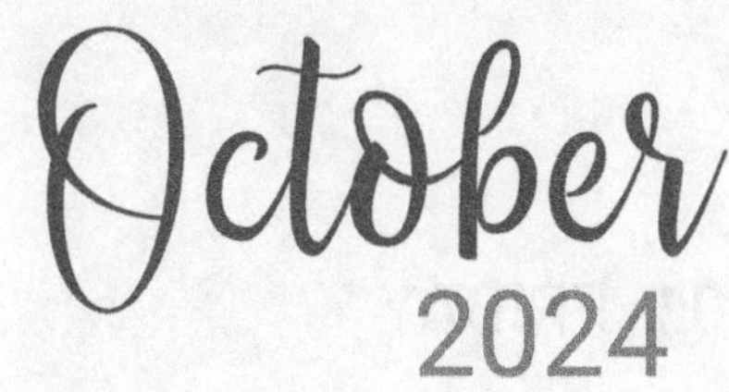

# October
## 2024

**29** TUESDAY

**30** WEDNESDAY

**31** THURSDAY

NOTES

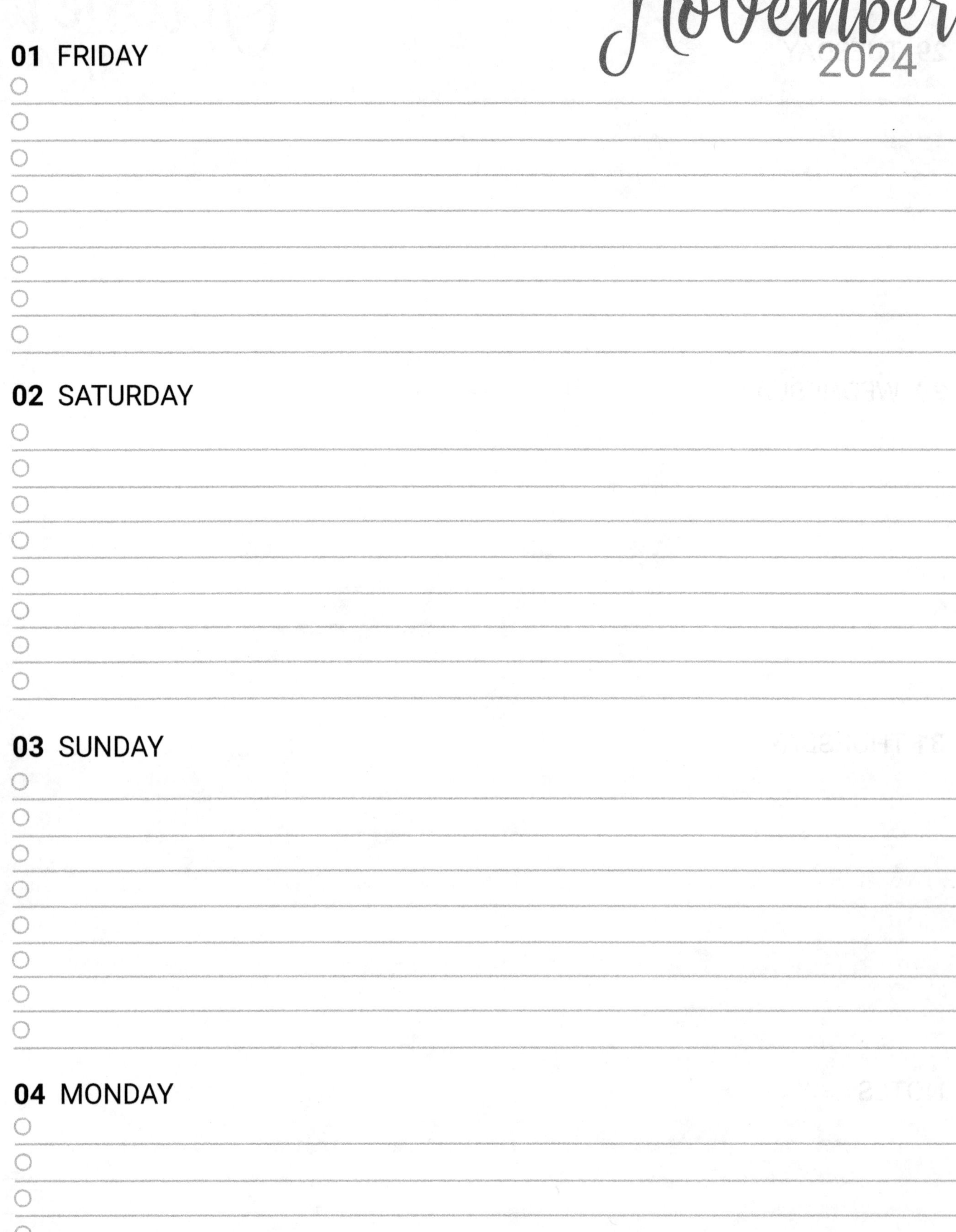

# November
## 2024

**01** FRIDAY

**02** SATURDAY

**03** SUNDAY

**04** MONDAY

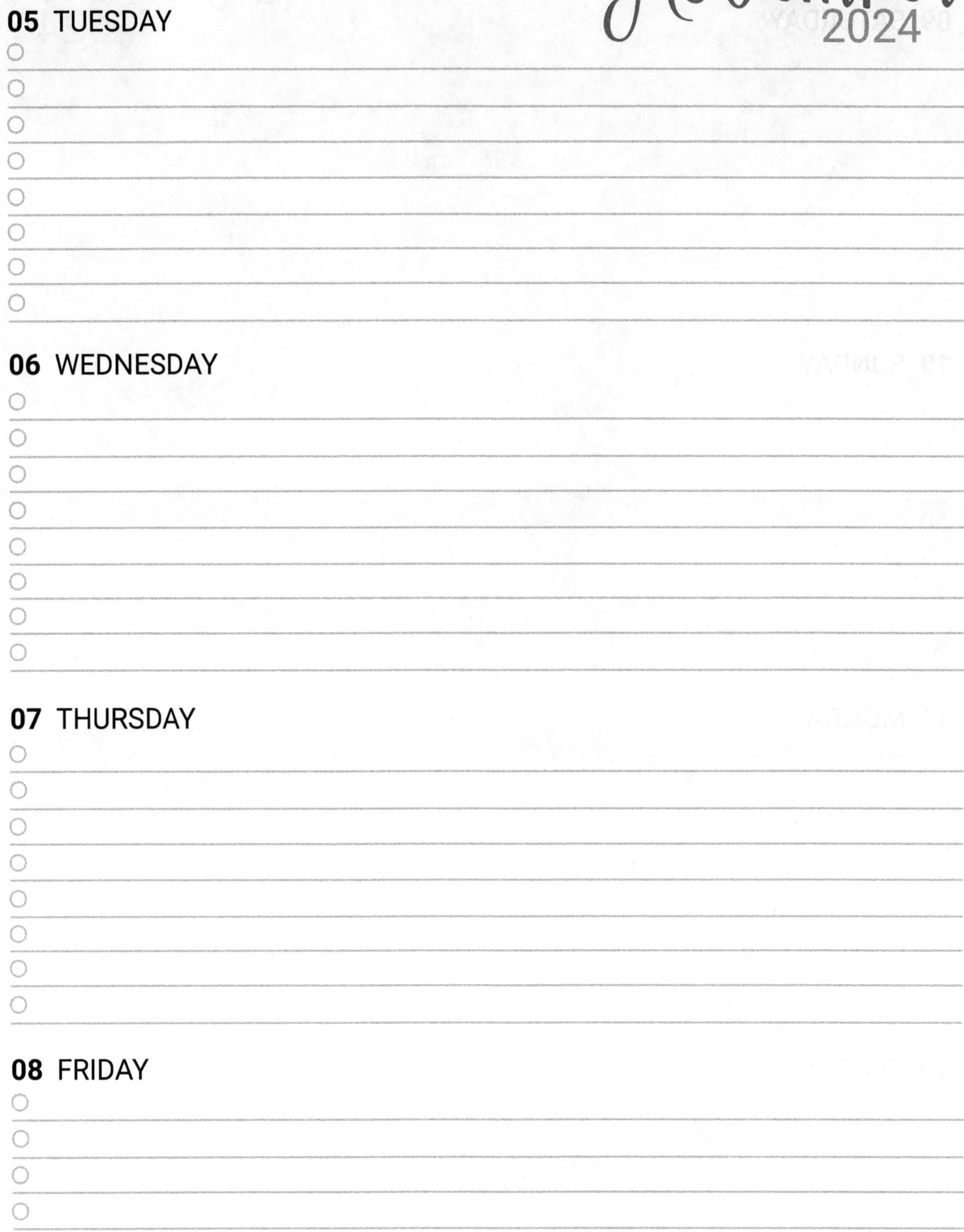

# November 2024

**05** TUESDAY

**06** WEDNESDAY

**07** THURSDAY

**08** FRIDAY

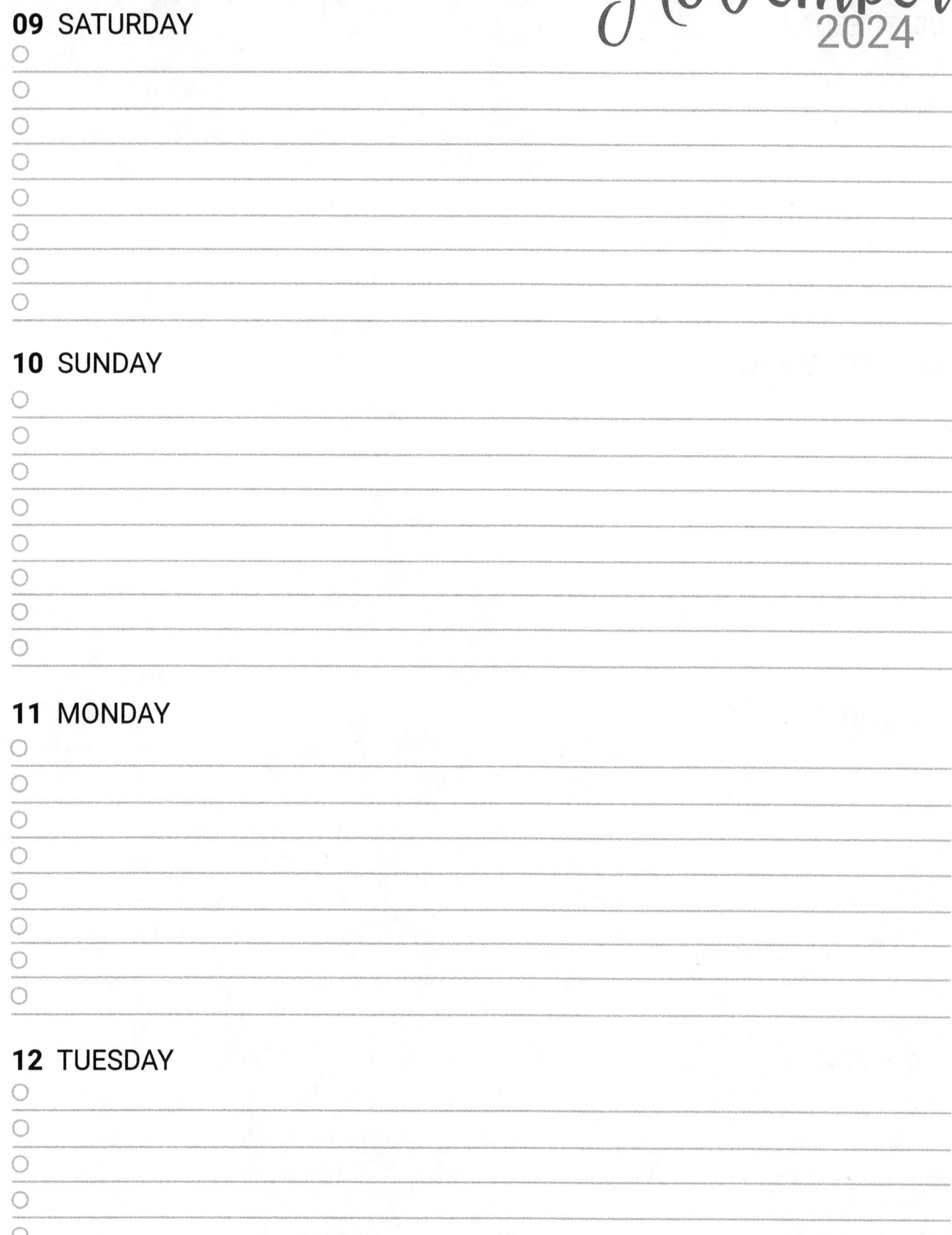


November
2024

09 SATURDAY

10 SUNDAY

11 MONDAY

12 TUESDAY

**13** WEDNESDAY

**14** THURSDAY

**15** FRIDAY

**16** SATURDAY

# November 2024

**17** SUNDAY

**18** MONDAY

**19** TUESDAY

**20** WEDNESDAY

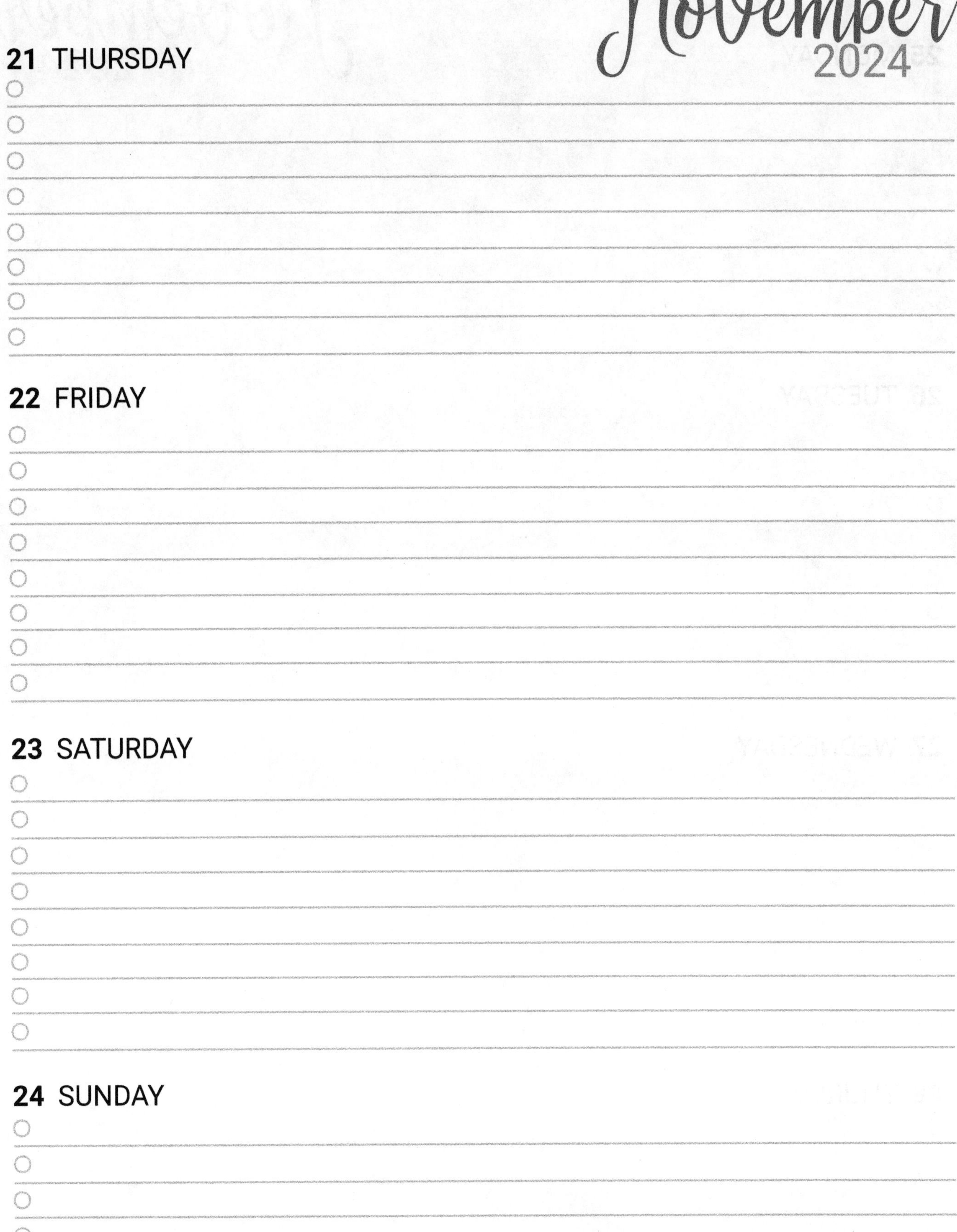



**21** THURSDAY

**22** FRIDAY

**23** SATURDAY

**24** SUNDAY

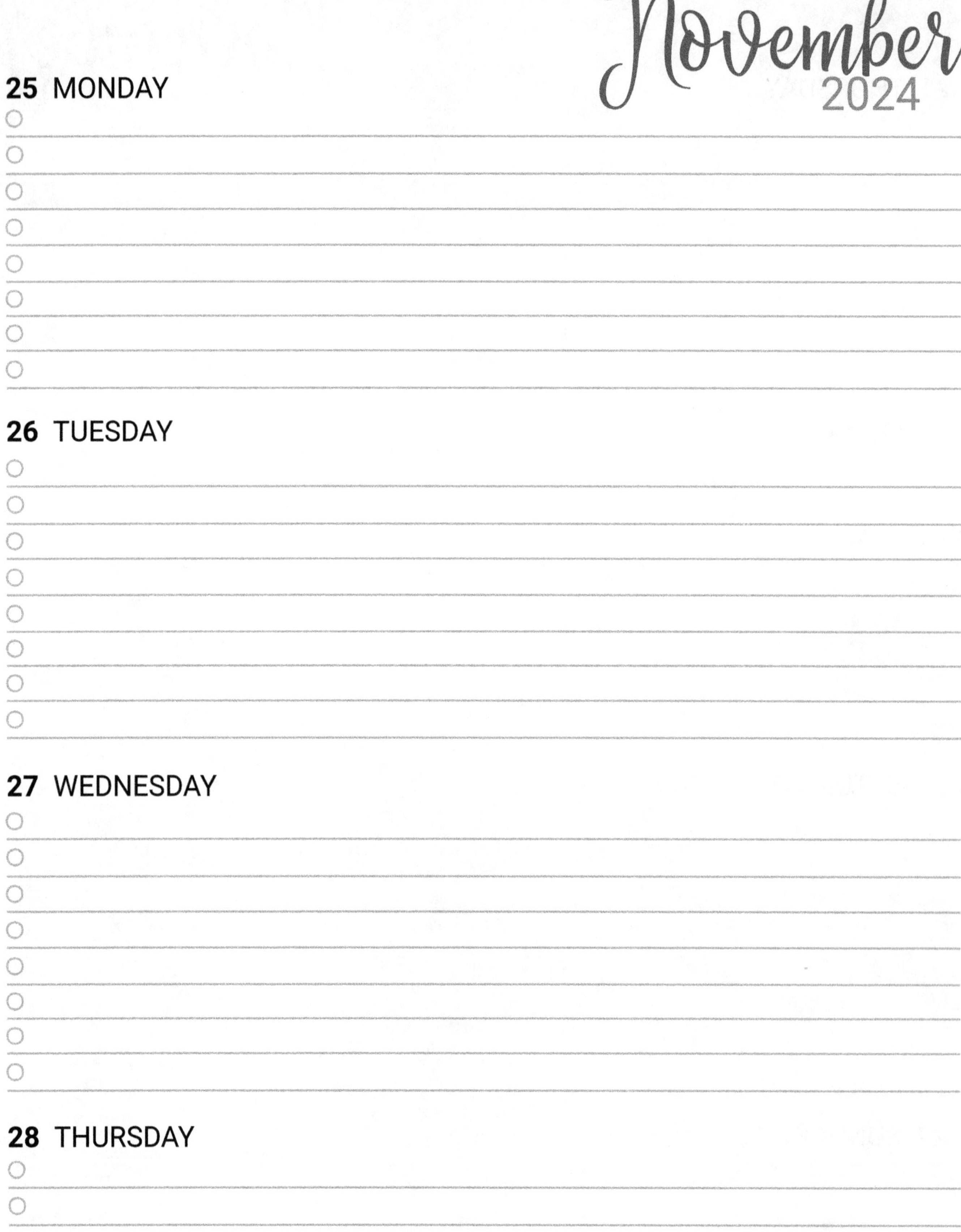



**25** MONDAY

**26** TUESDAY

**27** WEDNESDAY

**28** THURSDAY

**29** FRIDAY

**30** SATURDAY

NOTES

**01** SUNDAY

**02** MONDAY

**03** TUESDAY

**04** WEDNESDAY

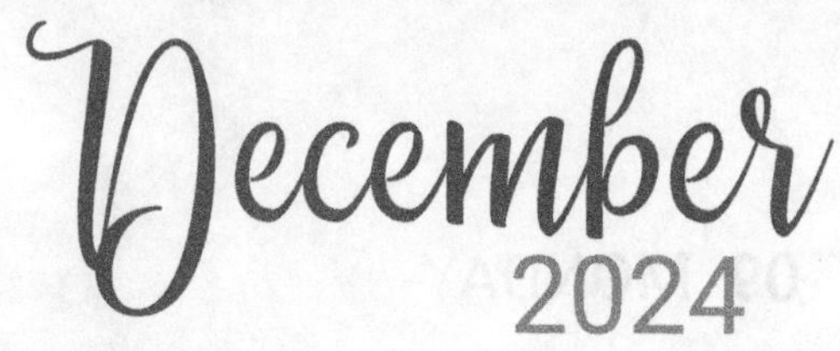


## 05 THURSDAY

## 06 FRIDAY

## 07 SATURDAY

## 08 SUNDAY

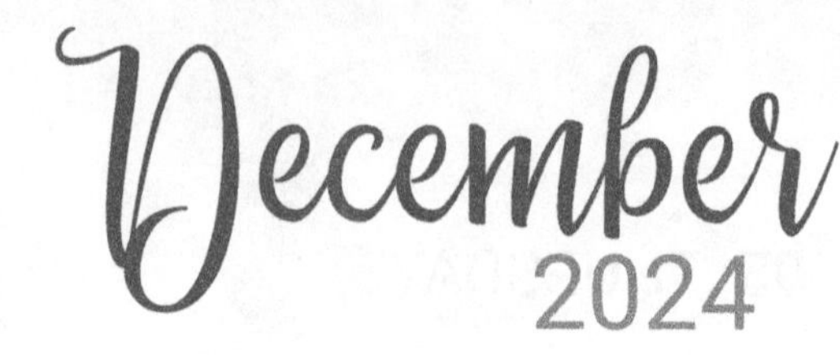


**09** MONDAY

**10** TUESDAY

**11** WEDNESDAY

**12** THURSDAY

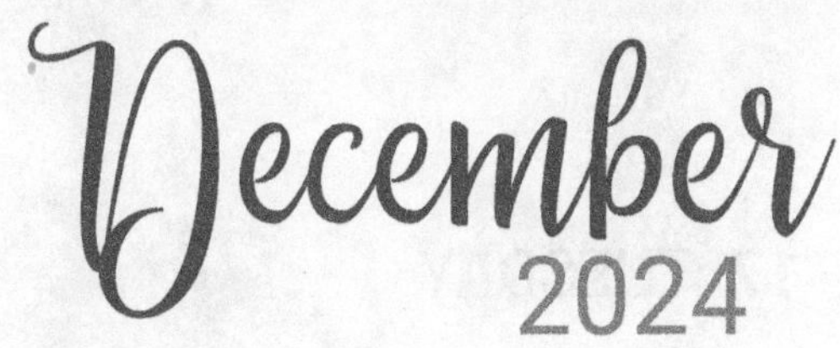

# December
## 2024

**13** FRIDAY

**14** SATURDAY

**15** SUNDAY

**16** MONDAY

**17** TUESDAY

**18** WEDNESDAY

**19** THURSDAY

**20** FRIDAY

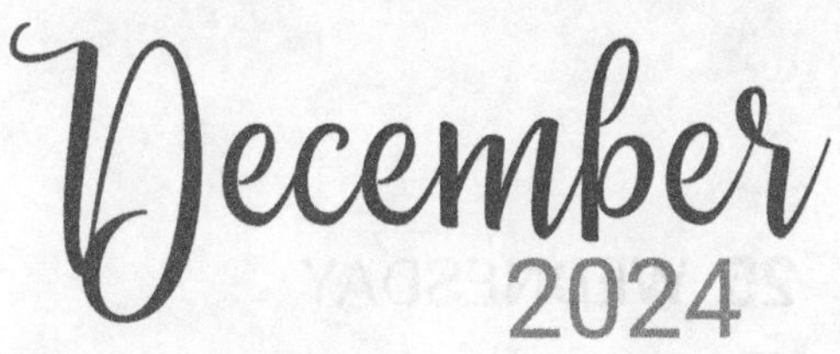

# December
## 2024

**21** SATURDAY

**22** SUNDAY

**23** MONDAY

**24** TUESDAY

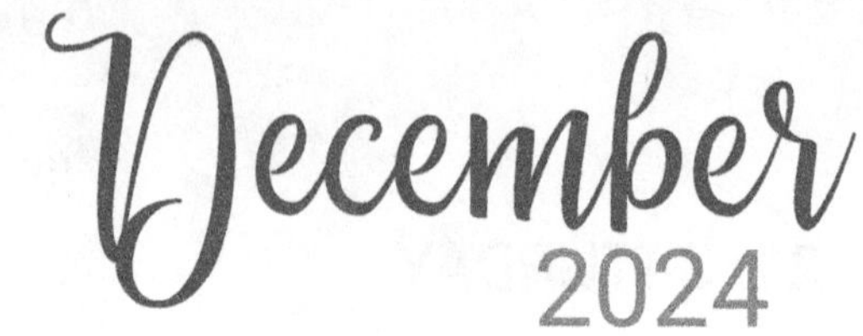



**25** WEDNESDAY

**26** THURSDAY

**27** FRIDAY

**28** SATURDAY

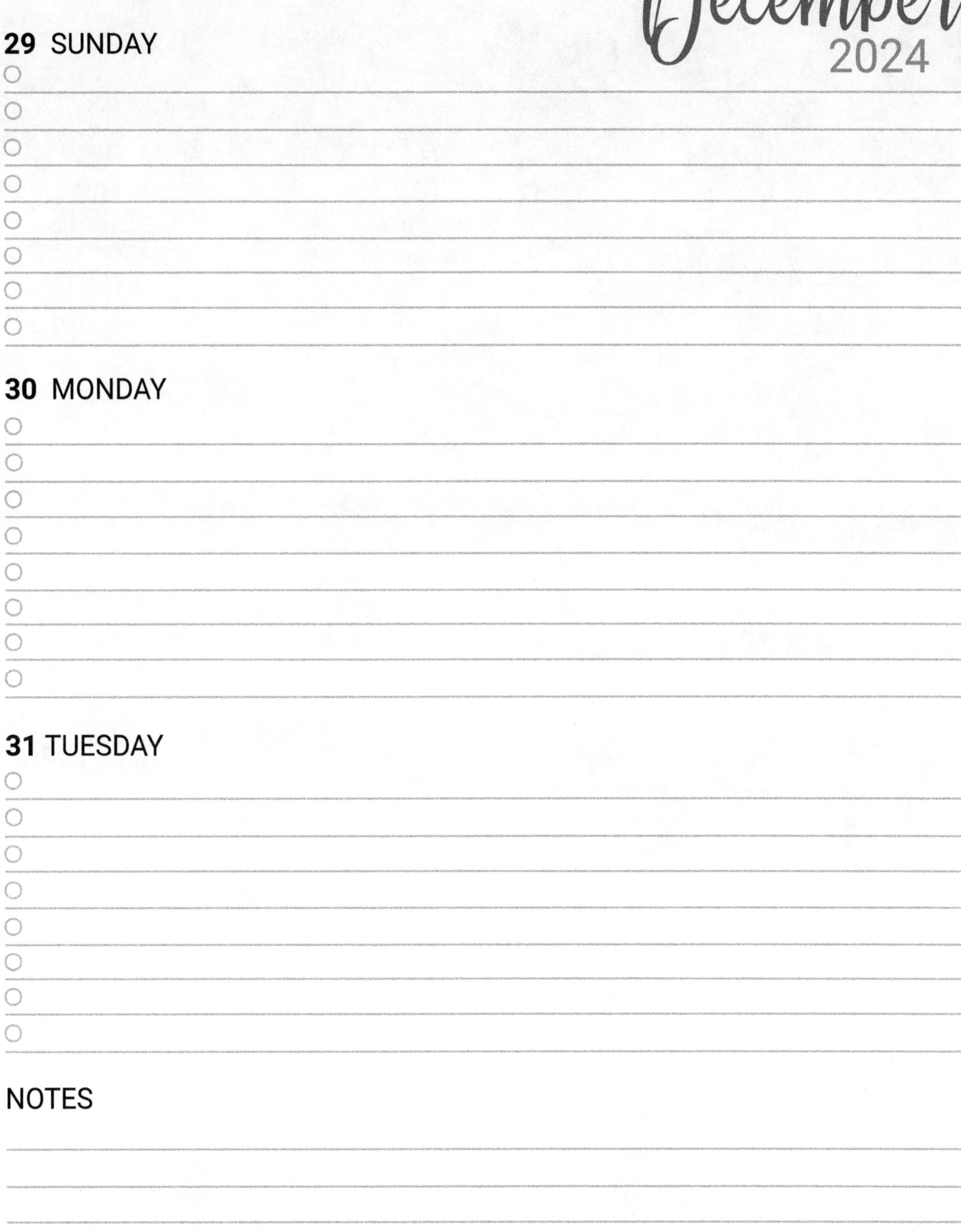

# December
## 2024

**29** SUNDAY

**30** MONDAY

**31** TUESDAY

**NOTES**